A Wynken, Blynken & Nod Adventure!

by L.A. Liechty

To all of those who love to dream…

The snow whirled and twirled outside. It glistened in the moonlight, and danced upon the windows. All the houses lay snuggled in the fresh blanket of snow, with fires crackling in the fireplaces and candles glistening on the windowsills. But from all the cozy houses, there was one that stood out from the rest; 326 Tassleberrie Drive. For around this house, glowed a soft, magical aura of light. Perhaps it was simply a reflection of the moon and the stars; or perhaps it was from the lights hanging on the roof. That's what most folks would say. But, for those who have learned to see with more than just their eyes, there might be another explanation. Perhaps, it is because this is where magic will come to visit tonight; at 326 Tassleberrie Drive...

Upstairs, Kyra, Christopher and Jaden burst from their room in excitement. All three, freshly changed into their pajamas, raced each other down the stairs.

"Come on!" yelled little Christopher, "It's time for the presents!"

They raced down to where three beautiful gifts lay waiting for them in front of the fireplace. There was a bright red one with Christopher's name on it, a flashy yellow one for Jaden, and one for Kyra, wrapped in a magical silver blue paper. All of them had big ribbons and the promise of a wondrous surprise inside.

Their grandparents smiled happily at the effect their gifts were having. Sipping their hot chocolate from the comfort of the sofa, they beamed.

"Go ahead, open them!" said Grandma.

"Yes, see what you got!" chimed Granddad.

They each sat by their gifts planning out the quickest way to open them. Christopher was the first to tare open his gift.

"Wow! A tractor Truck!" he cried, "That's amazing! Thanks Grandma & Granddad!"

"Oh cool! A remote control sports car!! Thanks!" hooted Jaden in such excitement that he stuffed the batteries in the wrong way.

While everyone else oohed and ahhed over the boys gifts, Kyra slowly unwrapped hers. Quite suddenly, a wisp of a glistening sparkle flew out from the gift in her hands, but then was gone. No one else saw it. It happened so fast that Kyra wondered if it was her imagination, for things like that couldn't really happen...could they?

Turning over her gift, Kyra looked to see a beautiful book in her hands. The color was a magical blue that almost seemed alive.

"A Wynken, Blynken and Nod Adventure," Kyra read out loud as she looked at the title.

The boys looked in silence for a moment then burst out laughing. "Ahh! A book?! You only got a dorky book! Ha, ha ha!" Christopher could not contain himself.

"Man, I'm glad I got this sports car and not a plain old book!" Jaden said as he turned his attention back to his new toy car.

Grandma smiled at Kyra, "It's not just a book." she said, "It's a doorway into a wonderful world."

"Don't underestimate this book," her Grandfather added, "for this book can take you to a very, very magical place."

"How?" asked Kyra.

With a hidden wisdom behind her Grandma's eyes she whispered, "You'll have to discover that for yourself."

Granddad looked over to the boys who were much more fascinated with their toy cars. "You boys would do well to discover the magic too," he said. The boys just snickered.

"Books are dumb," Jaden said.

"And boring," agreed Christopher.

Granddad looked back to Kyra with a wink. "Not this one," he said.

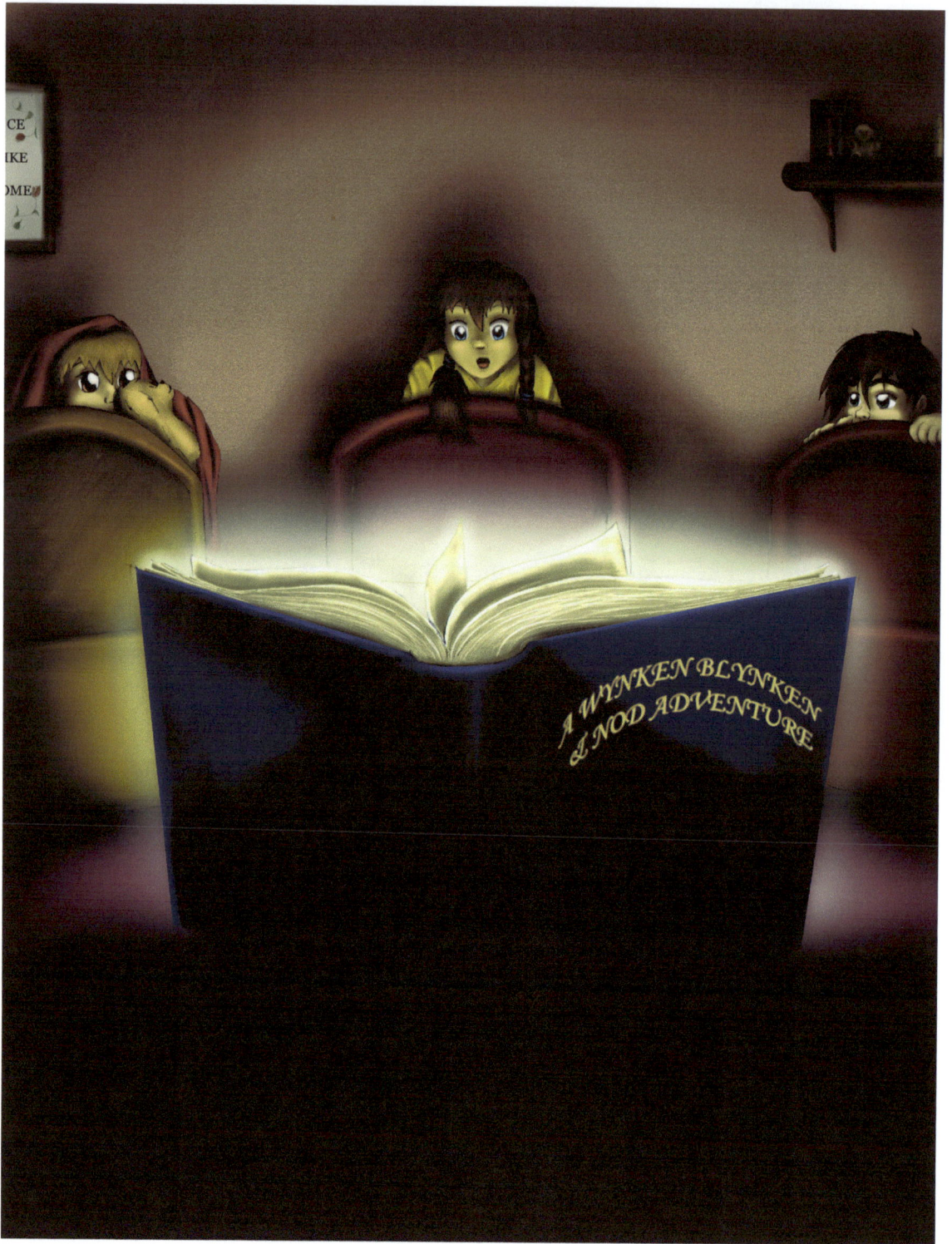

When bedtime was called that night, Christopher, Jaden and Kyra found it difficult to close their eyes and go to sleep. They all lay in their beds with their eyes wide open.

Then, something thumped on the floor.

"What was that?" asked Jaden.

They all sat up. No one knew, but whatever it was thumped again!

Peering over their beds to the floor, all three of them saw with astonishment that the magical blue book Kyra had gotten was moving. All by itself.

"Whoa," Jaden said quietly in disbelief.

"What's it doing?" Christopher managed to ask in a whisper.

Suddenly the book flipped up onto Kyra's bed and opened to the first page. A magical light streamed out of the book straight up to the ceiling. They stared in wonder. Then, popping out of the book with a crack appeared a little round creature of the likes Kyra had never seen before. The little creature had a big bright smile and a funny little voice.

"Hi Kyra! How's it going?" it asked.

Bewildered, all Kyra could think to say was, "Uhh...fine thanks."

Christopher peered over at the creature from under his covers and managed to make a peep.

"Who are you?" he asked.

The creature scowled a little, and with a frown turned to answer. "I'm sorry, did you say something to me? Cause I thought you called us dorky and boring, before!"

Christopher was stunned. "How did you know that?" he asked. Without an answer the little creature scowled at Jaden.

"And you called us dumb!" he barked in his little voice. Then came a second crack, and another little creature looking very similar to the first one, popped out of the book, munching on something that looked like a green carrot.

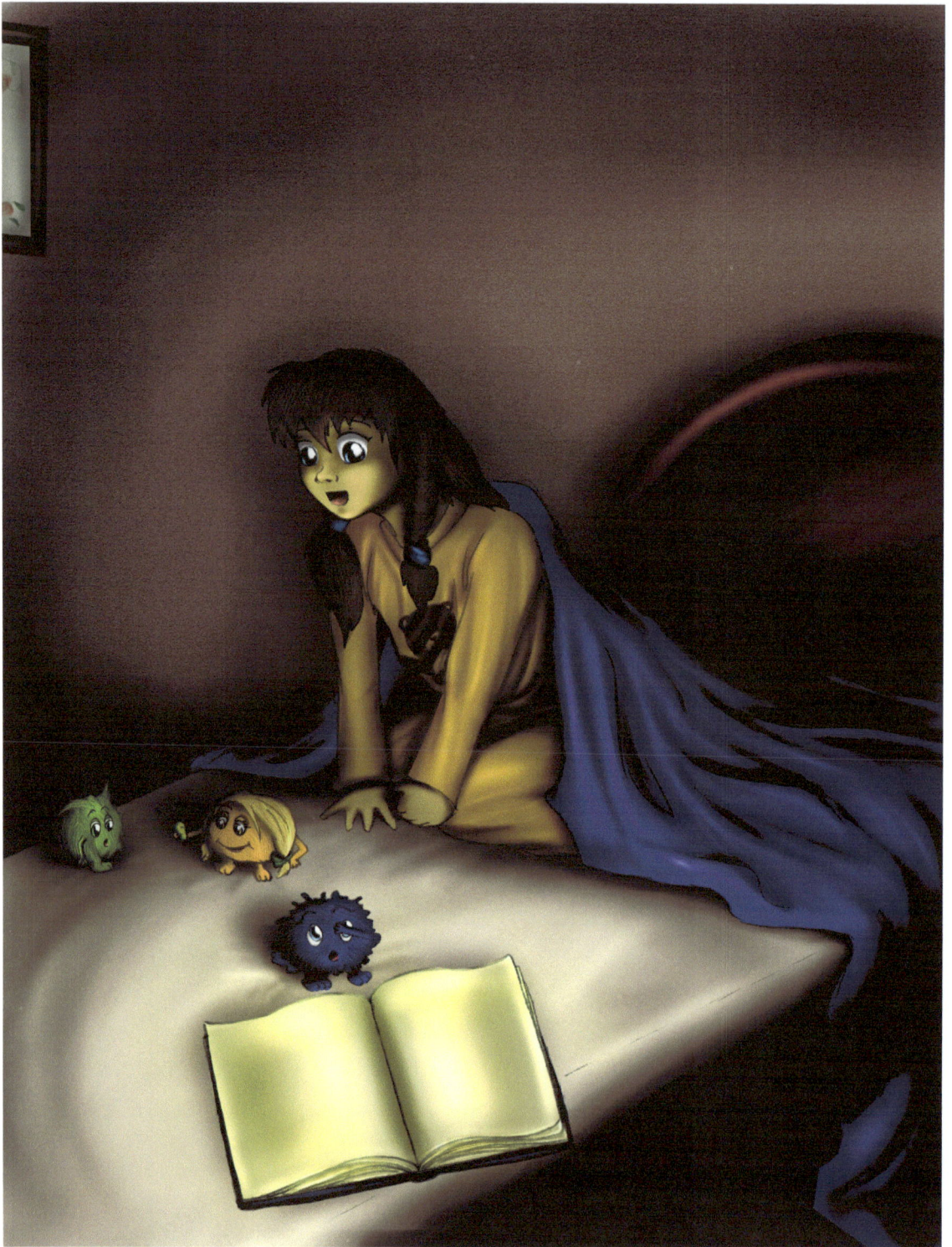

"Who you talking to Wynk?" it said in a voice that sounded like a tiny little woman.

"Nobody," Wynken said as he turned away from the boys who were still huddled under their blankets.   "Just talking to Kyra," he said in a pleasant tone.

"Oh, Hi Kyra! Didn't see you there behind Wynk's big old head." The other little creature pulled herself out of the book and plopped on the blanket next to Kyra, still munching on her little green carrot.

"Blynk, your head is just as big as mine!" Wynken was scowling again. As the two little creatures began to poke at each other, Kyra found her voice.

"Who are you?" she asked.

"Oh, right. We should introduce ourselves. I'm Wynken." He made a little bow.

"And I'm Blynken." Blynken said imitating the same bow.

"And this is…" Wynken stopped as he realized the third creature wasn't there. "Where is he?" Wynken was not pleased.

"He was right behind me," replied Blynken. She stuck her head inside the book. "Here he is," she said. Then, reaching in with her long arm, she pulled something out of the book. With a flop and a crack, a third creature appeared on Kyra's bed, looking sleepy and confused.

"Ouch! What'd you pull me so hard for, Blynk?" he said rubbing his head.

"Because your late!" shouted Wynken who promptly kicked him into standing with his fluffy foot. Wynken cleared his throat and finished the introductions, "And this is Nod."

"Nice to meet you Kyra!" Nod began his bow, but quickly lost his balance and fell over.

"How do you know my name?" Kyra asked as she helped Nod back up to his feet.

"Because someone who loves you very much has sent us to you," answered Wynken.

"Why?"

"Why…?" asked Wynken in confusion, "What do you mean why? Don't you know who we are?"

Kyra shook her head, "No," she answered.

Wynken, Blynken and Nod found themselves speechless. They couldn't believe it.

"How can that be?" asked Blynken.

"Don't you know the poem?" asked Nod.

"Don't you know the song?" asked Wynken.

"Don't you know the story?" all three asked.

Kyra simply shook her head and said again, "No."

"Well," declared Wynken, as he threw his hands on his hips. "This is just unacceptable!"

"We're definitely going to have to do something about this," agreed Blynken.

"That's right," interjected Nod, "No child should go without a Wynken, Blynken and Nod adventure." He turned to Wynken and Blynken, "We're going to have to take her in."

"Yep!" said Wynken.

"Without a doubt!" said Blynken. Kyra crinkled her nose in confusion.

"Take me where?" she asked, for she had no idea what they were talking about.

"Into the book of course!" Nod said.

"Into the book?" Kyra almost laughed. "That's impossible!"

Wynken covered Kyra's mouth with his hand, then looked around as if to make sure no one had heard her say these terrible words. "Quick, take it back!" Wynken insisted.

Kyra muffled her response from behind Wynken's hand, "But it *is* impossible" she said.

"No" said Blynken, "It's only impossible if you believe it's impossible! Think about it;

before tonight you would have thought it's impossible for three little creatures to pop out of a book, right? But here we are."

Kyra realized Blynken was right about that. "Well, that's true" she said.

"So you see, not everything you think is impossible really is impossible. Now quick, take it back, or you'll ruin everything!" Wynken insisted.

"Alright, I take it back. Maybe it is possible, but I'm curious how this is going to work" she said. In a breath of magic and a hint of mystery, the book began to glow. "Ooh..." whispered Kyra in amazement.

"Good, you fixed it" Wynken said in relief as he lowered his hand.

"That was close," Nod added. "You see Kyra, words like 'impossible' or 'can't' are the only words that can block the magic."

"Oh," said Kyra.

"Besides, it's total nonsense," added Wynken. "Nothing's impossible, you just don't know it yet." He smiled at Kyra.

The three little creatures circled the book and started to hum a little song. A fountain of bright sprinkles and sparkles raced up from the book all the way to the ceiling. It encircled Kyra's bed and danced before her eyes. Wynken glanced at Kyra. "You ready?" he asked.

"For what exactly?" Kyra asked.

"For the best adventure you've ever had!" Wynken answered. Christopher and Jaden were on the edges of their beds, in awe of the magic happening by Kyra. "Hey, what about us?" asked Christopher.

"Yeah, we want to come too!" called Jaden.

Blynken shot them a nasty little look. "You can't come. Non believers in the greatness of books are not allowed to come!" she said firmly.

"Ahh, come on. Let us come too!" said Jaden. "Please let us come. We want an adventure too!"

"Do you take it back?" asked Wynken.

"Yes! Yes, we do!" cried Christopher and Jaden.

"Really and truly take it back?" Wynken asked.

"Yes. Really and truly," they said.

Wynken hesitated, and then smiled, "Alright, then hop on board!"

With a glee of excitement, Christopher and Jaden jumped onto Kyra's bed as it bumped and thumped.   Suddenly, it started to lift up off the floor!

Christopher peered over the side, "Wow! Cool!" He said.

Jaden held on as the bed made a last bump off the floor. "Are we flying?"

"No," said Wynken, "we are sailing…!"

The bed suddenly changed its form and turned into a big, wooden shoe with a tall sail. The sparkles and lights brushed like waves up against the sides of the shoe and they began to sail. The book opened up like a giant door and the sparkling waves pulled the wooden shoe through. Kyra, Christopher and Jaden held on as they sailed into a wondrous world they had never known...

Wynken, Blynken and Nod one night
Sailed off in a wooden shoe
Sailed on a river of crystal light
Into a sea of dew

"Where are you going and what do you wish?"
The old moon asked the three
"We have come with our silver-gold nets,
To fish in your beautiful sea"
Replied the fishermen three
Wynken, Blynken & Nod

The old moon laughed and sang a song
As they rocked in their wooden shoe
And the wind that sped them all night long
Ruffled the waves of dew

The stars in the sky were the Herring fish
Sought by the fishermen three
"So cast your nets where ever you wish,
Never afeared are we!"
They sang to the fishermen three
Wynken, Blynken & Nod...

Wynken, Blynken and Nod continued to sing, (though terribly out of tune and repeating only the lines of the songs that had their names in it) and a magical world unfolded around them as they sailed through. There were beautiful waterfalls that sparkled and glistened. Fish that could swim in and out of the water in all shapes, colors and sizes. Across the water on the shore were horses with wings and long flowing manes.   There were small creatures that looked like elves picking fruits and flowers off of talking trees.

The smiling moon lit the sky in a calm milk white light as little fairy bells lit the paths for the elves and small furry creatures to cross.

Kyra and Blynken laughed and talked with the moon. Jaden was busy untangling himself from one of the silver/gold nets that Wynken tried to cast overboard. Christopher was peering over the side of the boat at a stunning white fish in the magical water

"Hey, look at this funny little fish!" he shouted with a giggle.

The (not so little) fish popped out of the water, nose-to-nose with Christopher.

"A fish?!" He scowled, "You think I'm just a measly little fish?" He lifted his fin and flicked it across the end of Christopher's nose.

"Ouch!" he said as he rubbed his nose. "What'd you do that for?"

The white fish marched through the air up to the bow of the boat.

"I will have you know, I am no little fish! I am Zook the Fearless Carp and I am very special. I am in charge of these waters because I am the bravest and fastest Carp in this whole ocean!" He folded his fins across his chest and wrinkled his nose proudly.

Wynken leaned over, "He's the ONLY carp in this whole ocean," he whispered.

"Popalapop!" barked Zook, as he skipped over the fact that that was actually true. "Now, I am in charge here, so, who are you and what are you doing here?" he snipped.

Wynken waddled over to Zook. "Ahh, come on Zook. It's us! You know us we are here all the time." he pleaded.

"Yeah, Zookie, you don't really need to see the paper work do you? We've been through this a hundred times," Blynken added.

Zook shot his fin up in the air to stop her.

"What a mess would it be if everyone would criss cross this ocean as they pleased? No!" he yelled. "This is not proper procedure. Your papers must be in order! Give me!" He held his fin out. His eyes remained closed to ignore any more attempts at passing without his permission.

"Ok Nod," Wynken yelled over to Nod, who was busy steering the wooden shoe through the waters. "You were in charge of the paperwork this time so bring it over. Mr. attitude here wants to see it even though we've shown him the same thing every time we've come through here."

Zook simply opened the corner of his eye to peer at him. "Papers please," he ordered.

Nod ran over to Zook with a messy pile of papers in his hands, but just as he was about to get close enough to hand them to Zook, he tripped. The papers flew out of his hands and landed in a big mess at Zook's bottom fins.

"Oh, boy," Zook said with a tired exhale.

"Nod, you nincompoop!" Wynken said.

"Well, it was already a mess when I found them from last time, Wynken, so this is your fault."

"No, last time was Blynken's responsibility!" Wynken snapped back.

"Your papers are not in order!" barked Zook.

As the four of them argued back and forth about the papers, Kyra, Christopher and Jaden noticed the wooden shoe was rocking a little more rough than before. Kyra looked back at the steering wheel and realized that no one was steering the shoe!

"Excuse me," she tried to say, but the argument had grown so loud that none of them could hear her. She tried again a little louder.

"Excuse me," but still, no one answered her.

Christopher took a deep breath and yelled, "Hey!" That got their attention and they all looked at   Christopher. "Who's driving the shoe?" he asked.

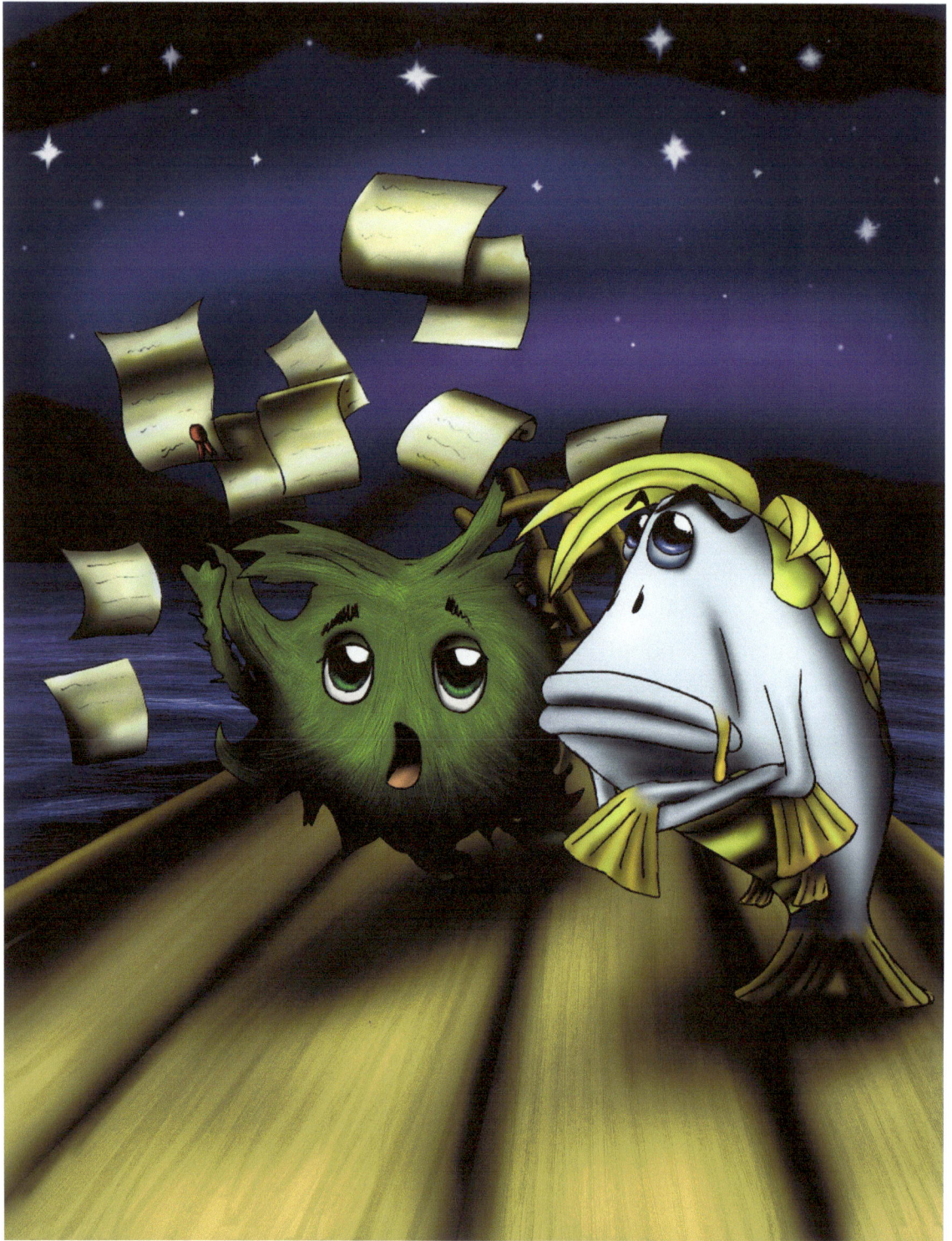

As the jaws dropped one at a time, Wynken, Blynken, Nod and Zook all realized with shock that the shoe had been drifting into darker and deeper waters. Suddenly, the shoe hit something hard and stopped with a smash and a thump! Everyone on board flew over the front of the shoe and landed on the murky ground.

"Where are we?" asked Kyra.

"It's really dark here," Christopher said.

"Yeah, and cold," added Jaden.

Zook noticed a big hole that was now in the front of the wooden shoe. "Mm Mmm…your boat is not in order," He declared.

"You know," said Blynken as she carefully kicked around in the dirt, "this kind of reminds me of Scary Land Island."

"Oh no!" exclaimed Zook, his voice shaking with fear.

"Ooh…" whispered Wynken and Nod as they huddled together, "No, please say it isn't."

"Why?" asked Christopher, "What is 'Scary Land Island'?"

The fear on Wynken and Nod's face made Christopher shiver. Out of the blue, there was a loud howl and a screech! Everyone jumped at the startling noise.

Zook tried to sound calm as he explained, "We call this place Scary Land Island cause it's the home of Blorg!"

"What's a Blorg?" asked Jaden.

"Not a what, a who," corrected Wynken. "Blorg is a monster!"

"Yeah, a huge one with big teeth and sharp claws!" shuddered Blynken. "He's a mean one, Blorg is."

"What if he eats us all?!" Zook said as he trembled in fright. There was another loud crash and the ground shook with big, heavy thumps of monster feet! Everyone jumped and Zook let out a screech of fear. Then, a big, shadow crept out of the dark cave behind them.

"It's Blorg!" whispered Wynken in a quiver. They gasped in fright.

"What do we do?" whispered Kyra.

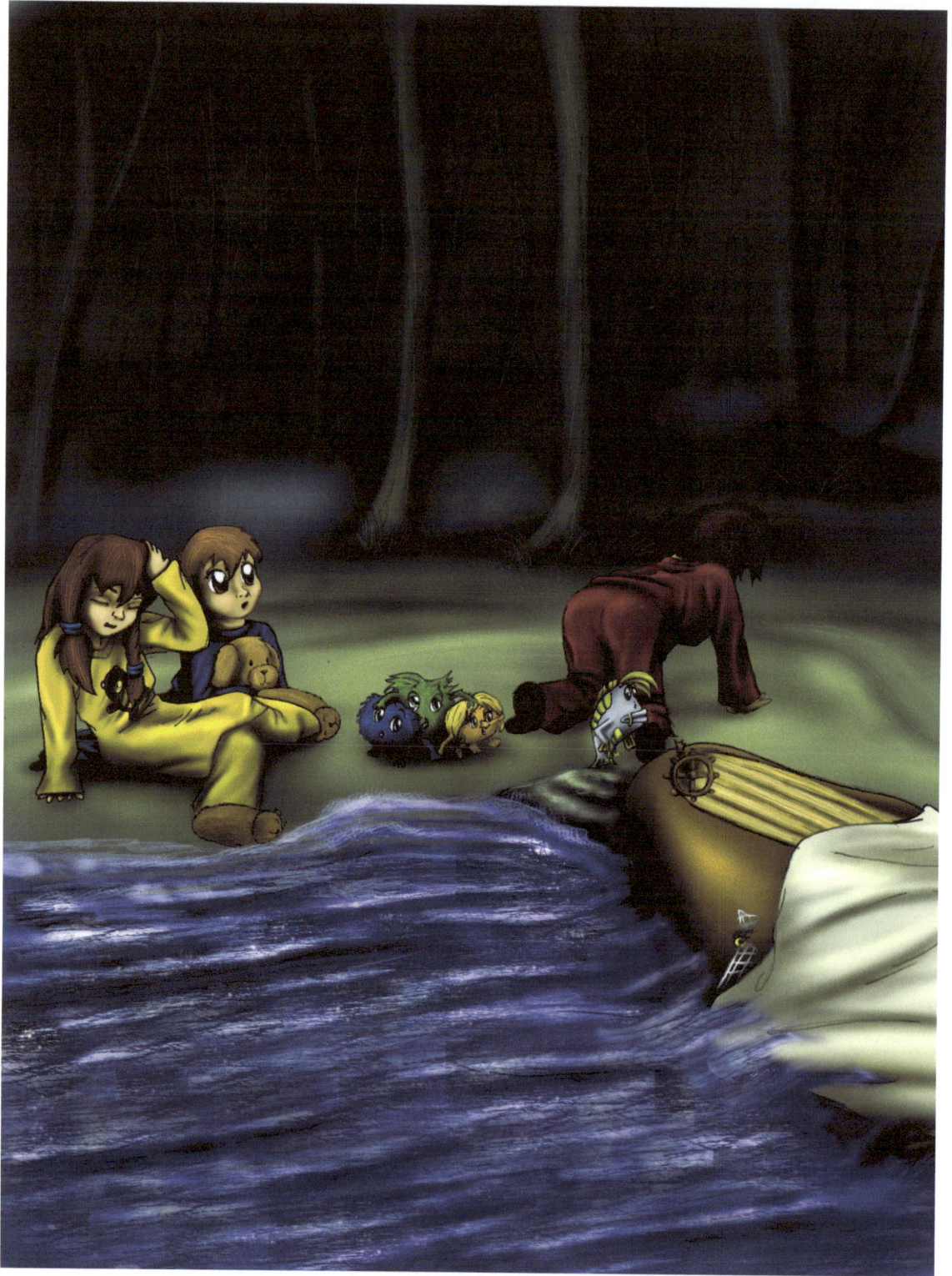

But before anyone could answer, Blorg was upon them! Blorg was the most gigantic thing they had ever seen. He opened his huge, grumpy looking mouth, showing that he had more sharp, pointed teeth then they could count. And then, Blorg roared! Everyone screamed.

"Run!" yelled Wynken. Kyra ran to the left of Blorg. Wynken, Blynken and Nod to the right. Christopher and Jaden saw an opening between the creature's big legs and ran straightforward. But Zook couldn't run. He was too scared and his little fish fins just wouldn't move. Blorg reached down and grabbed Zook in one of his big claws. He pulled him up close to his eyes and peered at him.

"Blorg's got Zook!" Cried Kyra.

"Oh no!" They all watched in horror. With his other big hand, Blorg picked up the Wooden Shoe, as if it were as light as a feather. Then, with a crunch and a thud of his feet, he started back to his cave; with Zook and the Wooden Shoe trapped in his claws.

"What do we do?" Cried Jaden.

"Shouldn't we just run away?" Nod quivered.

"No! We've got to help Zook!" insisted Kyra.

"And we can't leave this island without our shoe," said Wynken.

"But Blorg is so big and powerful. How in the world can we save Zook and get the Shoe back?" questioned Christopher. "We're too small to fight him."

The Moon, who had been watching from above, spoke in a deep voice. "Maybe you don't need to *fight* him," he said.

"How else can we do it? He's so mean," said Christopher.

"And so scary! Why is he so scary?" Blynken whimpered.

"He's a Blorg, and when Blorg's aren't happy, they can seem very mean and scary," said the Moon.

"What can we do?" asked Wynken.

"The only way you will be able to save Zook and get your shoe back is if you can find a way to help Blorg feel happy. Then, maybe, he will let Zook go and give you back your shoe," answered the Moon.

"But that's imposs-" Kyra stopped herself from saying 'impossible,' for she remember the first lesson Wynken, Blynken and Nod taught her; and they had been right.

"Mmm," she said as she wondered, "Is there a way to help Blorg feel happy?" Kyra asked the Moon.

"There is only one person who knows the answer to that. You must ask the Fairy Queen," he said.

"Where can we find her?" asked Jaden.

"Follow the secret path down to the waters edge. Once you are there, call her name three times. She will come to you – but only if you believe," said the Moon.

"If we believe?" asked Kyra.

"Yes. She will only show herself to those who truly have the power to believe; for her time is precious and her secrets wondrous. Only a special few have ever seen her; the ones who have the power to believe inside them. If you have this, she will come and help you."

"But I don't have any power inside me," Christopher sad sadly.

"Oh, but you do little Christopher. And so do you Kyra. And you Jaden. You all have the power inside you, or else you wouldn't have made it here in the first place. Just close your eyes and concentrate," the Moon said.

"OK," they said, "We'll do it."

"How do we find the secret path?" asked Christopher.

The moon blew down a pearly ray of light and a mystical path appeared. They followed the winding path down to the waters edge in search of the Fairy Queen who could help them save Zook and get their Shoe back.

Once they arrived, the path disappeared and they stood by the water.

"OK," said Kyra, "this is it. Everyone believe." They all closed their eyes and concentrated.

"Ready?" asked Kyra.

"Ready" they all answered.

"OK, on the count of three. One, two, -"

Then, on three, they all called out, "Fairy Queen, Fairy Queen, Fairy Queen!" But nothing happened. Kyra opened her eyes.

"It didn't work," she announced.

"Who didn't believe?" asked Wynken.

"Maybe we just didn't believe enough" answered Jaden, "Let's try again."

"Yeah, and everyone really concentrate on believing," agreed Kyra.

They closed their eyes, and this time, they believed with all their might.

"One, two – "

"Fairy Queen, Fairy Queen, Fairy Queen!" they cried.

At first it was quiet, then, something happened. The wind stirred, the waves ruffled, and the sea that was still began to bubble. They opened their eyes.

Before them, just above the water, swirled an amazing bluish green mist. As the mist flowed out, the colors changed to red purple and peach. Then, from the middle of the mist came the most beautiful Fairy Queen they could have ever imagined.

"Hello," she said. Her voice sparkled. "I'm the Fairy Queen of the Lollipop Sea. You have called me, what can I do for you?"

They told the tale of what happened to Zook and their wooden shoe, and what the Moon had said about Blorg's unhappiness. The Fairy Queen listened intently.

"We thought if we could help Blorg get happy again, he would let Zook go, and give us back our Wooden Shoe," Kyra explained, "but we don't know how. Can you help us?"

The Fairy Queen pondered the question and replied, "Yes, I think there is a way, but it wont be easy" she said. "Have you ever heard of the Sugar Plum Tree?"

They all shook their heads; none of them had ever heard of such a thing. "I shall tell you the tale of The Sugar-Plum Tree, and take you to it. Perhaps you can discover a way to use the magic you find there." She said. "It lies on the other side of the Island."

There was another rump and tumble from Blorg's cave and they all shuddered. "We must go quickly. Blorg may be coming after you, and he is very fast. I suggest we fly." The Fairy Queen said.

"But we aren't magical, Fairy Queen, and we don't have any wings," Kyra explained, "We can't fly."

The Fairy Queen gave a little wink, "You don't need wings to fly, my dear," and with a wave of her hand appeared three magical creatures flying up out of the sea. There was a Seahorse with a shimmering mane of gold, a bright red Octopus with twenty-three tentacles, and a yellow and green Sea Turtle with six fins and a long tail. Everyone found themselves sitting in the pillowy saddles ready for the journey. The Fairy Queen sat atop a beautiful, angle/white unicorn with gigantic wings. As they lifted to the air, the Fairy Queen began the tale of the wondrous secrets that very few have ever known; the magical secrets of The Sugar-Plum Tree...

Have you ever heard of the Sugarplum Tree?
'Tis a marvel of great renown
It blooms on the shore of the lollipop sea
In the garden of Shut Eye Town

The fruit that it bares is so wonderfully sweet
As those who have tasted it say
And the magic says you have only to eat
Of that fruit to be happy next day

The Sugarplum Tree,
The Sugarplum Tree
The Sugarplum Tree

When you've got to the tree
You would have a hard time
To capture the fruit which I sing
For the tree is so tall
That no person could climb
To the boughs where
The Sugarplums swing

But up in the tree sits a chocolate cat
And the gingerbread dog prowls below
And this is the way
You contrive to get at
Those sugarplums tempting you so

Up in the Sugarplum Tree
The Sugarplum Tree
The Sugarplum Tree

You say but the word
To that gingerbread dog
And he barks with such
A terrible zest
That the chocolate cat
Is at once all agog
As her movements now will attest

And the chocolate cat
goes cavorting around
From this leafy limb onto that
And the Sugar-Plums tumble,
Of course, to the ground
Hurray for the chocolate cat

Here come The Sugarplums
Here come the Sugarplums...

There are marshmallows,
Gumdrops
And peppermint canes
With strippings
Of scarlet and gold

And you carry away,
From the treasure
That rains
As much as your
Dear arms can hold

So come my sweet
As the night draws near
And the magic
Starts to sprinkle down
And I'll rock you away
To The Sugar-Plum Tree
In the garden
Of Shut Eye Town

The Sugarplum Tree
The Sugarplum Tree...

"Now you know the power of the Sugar-Plums," The Fairy Queen said, "For they will make anyone, or anything, happy. You only need to eat one."

"But how do we get big old Blorg to eat one?" asked Nod.

"You must figure that out. But, someone else is calling me now, and I must go. You must hurry, for it does not take long for Blorg to cross the island and my guess is he is looking for you. Good luck my friends." And with that, the Fairy Queen waved her hands. She and her magical creatures disappeared behind the mysterious mist.

Blynken sat down under the tree in thought.

"This is going to take some planning," she said, "Blorg doesn't usually eat fruit, no matter how good it tastes." She rubbed her chin and wondered.

"Well, we better figure it out fast. Look!" Wynken pointed to the East. "Here comes Blorg!"

Blorg, who had followed the scent of their trail, was thundering down the hill towards them. His mouth was wide open in a roar just as ferocious as before. Looking at Blorg's big, open mouth gave Christopher an idea.

"Quick! Everyone into the tree! Grab some Sugar-Plums on the way!" he said.

When Blorg reached the tree he stopped. He sniffed in the air with his nose. He scanned around with his eyes, for he knew they were there, but he couldn't see them inside the big tree.

Christopher whispered to the others, "Wait till he roars again, then when his mouth opens, throw the Sugar-Plums in."

"Great idea Christopher," said Wynken.

So they waited, and waited, but Blorg didn't roar.

"What do we do now?" asked Nod.

It was Kyra who had an idea next.

"I'll jump down right on his foot. Then when he screams you guys throw the Sugar-Plums," she said.

"No, don't Kyra," shrieked Nod, "what if he catches you?"

"If we don't do something soon, he'll catch all of us!" she answered in a confident voice. "Get ready!"

Without even counting to three, Kyra jumped down. She landed hard, right on Blorg's big foot. Just as she thought, Blorg opened his mouth wide and roared.

"Now!" Kyra yelled as she dashed out of the way.

They all began to throw the Sugar-Plums. Christopher missed and hit Blorg's cheek. Wynken, Blynken and Nod, who all had terrible aim, missed completely. Nod didn't even get his to hit Blorg at all, and Wynken's Sugar-Plum went off to the left somewhere behind a banana-bread bench.

Blynken was so startled by all the throwing that she just dropped hers to the ground. Jaden was the only one who still had a Sugar-Plum to throw. He concentrated and then threw the Sugar-Plum. Bullseye! It went right into Blorg's mouth and down his throat. Blorg immediately stopped his roar. He licked his lips. He tilted his head to the left, then to the right. What was this magical thing he had just tried? Then something wondrous happened. Blorg started to smile. His sharp, jagged teeth peeked out, but they didn't look so frightening now that they were behind a soft smile.

Blorg looked at Kyra and blinked, then his eyes found the others who were still huddled in the tree. They all froze. Was Blorg still mean? Would he eat everyone? Slowly, Blorg's mouth started to open. Everyone got ready for another loud, horrible roar, but instead, all that came out was, "Can I have another one?"

His voice was deep and heavy, but nothing like the voice of a monster. Kyra picked up one of the Sugar-Plums that missed, "Here Blorg. You can have this one if you like," she said carefully.

Blorg took the plum from Kyra and held it in his great, big claws.

"Is it...a Sugar-Plum?" Blorg asked as he looked at it questioningly.

"Yes," replied Kyra.

Blorg's eyes filled with emotion, „I've always wanted to try a Sugar-Plum, but I never knew how to get them off the branches" he admitted quietly. He dropped his head down in sadness.

"I'm so big, and strong, but I could never get one down, and no one ever helped me." Blorg slumped to the ground with a thud and a tear rolled from his eye.

Wynken hopped out of the tree and approached Blorg cautiously.

"Why wouldn't anybody help you?" Wynken asked.

Blorg didn't look up, but answered with his head down.

"Because everyone is scared of me," Another tear dropped from his eye. "It's not nice when no one likes you. You guys are all friends, but I'm all alone," he sniffed.

Kyra walked up to Blorg and placed her hand on top of his.

"Is that why you've been unhappy, Blorg?" she asked sympathetically.

Blorg nodded his head.

Nod jumped down from the tree, his fear gone. "Well, we're not frightened of you Blorg. Not anymore," he said.

Christopher and Jaden jumped down too. Blynken wanted to jump down, but caught her foot and, instead, fell out of the tree. They encircled Blorg and reached out to him.

"We'll be your friends Blorg," Christopher said, "and we'll help you get the Sugar-Plums,"

Blorg lifted his head with a faint smile, „Really?"

"Yeah, we know the secret of how to get the plums down from the tree," encouraged Jaden. "We'll show you how."

Blorg was touched at their kindness, for he had never known kindness before.

"You will? You'll help me after I scared you so?" he asked through a few sniffs.

"Of course we will!" said Wynken, "But, could you do something for us? Could you let Zook go. He's just a little fish. I know he's got a big mouth and some attitude issues, but he's our friend and he's a good guy."

Blorg reached in his pocket and pulled out Zook, dangling him carefully in his big claws.

"Here he is," Blorg said, "I wasn't going to hurt him. I just always wanted a little fish."

Hanging upside down, Zook frowned, "I am no little fish! I am Zook the Fearless Carp. I am the bravest Carp in this whole ocean! Now put me down you big Blorg!" Zook barked.

Blorg opened his claw and dropped Zook. After a bounce or two on his little fish bottom, he sat up.

"You!" Zook said, his face was red with anger. With a huff, Zook marched over to Blorg with his fin in a fist. "I hit you with my fin!" he barked. "You big, mean, overgrown, dirty, rotten…," but he was cut off when   Wynken stuffed a Sugar-Plum in his mouth.

Zook stopped in his little fish tracks. He munched. Then he crunched. Then he swallowed the delicious fruit down. Licking his fish lips and cocking his head he looked up at Blorg who was smiling.

"Man," Zook said, "your teeth are not in order." With a smile and a jolly tone Zook continued, "But other than that, I must say, you have a very nice smile."

Zook climbed on the back of Blorg's hand. "Up Please," Zook instructed. Blorg lifted his hand, like an elevator, so Zook could look him in the eyes.

"So, I must properly introduce myself. I am Zook the Fearless Carp, I'm sure you have heard of me, my big furry pal," Blorg shrugged his shoulders, only knowing what Zook had already told him.

"You are the bravest Carp in this whole ocean?" he repeated.

"He's the ONLY carp in this whole ocean!" Wynken, Blynken and Nod corrected.

"Popalapop!" Zook stated.

"Are you the only one of your kind too?" asked Blorg sympathetically.

Deciding to be honest, Zook lowered his eyes, "Well…yes. I am."

"So am I," admitted Blorg.

Zook raised his fish eyes to Blorg.

"Really? We are both the only ones of our kind here?"

Blorg noded, and a big smile crept across Zook's fish lips. He wasn't the only one anymore who knew what it was like to feel alone. "Then Blorg, my friend, you and I are the bravest of our kinds! We are special. And Blorg, my furry giant, we are friends." Zook held out his little fin and Blorg tapped it with the end of his claw.

"Friends!" exclaimed Blorg.

"Now, how about those Sugar-Plums, Blorgy old pal?!" said Wynken.

Blorg let out a glee of excitement.

"Ok Blorg, here is the trick," explained Christopher, "You see that gingerbread dog over there? He is the key to getting the plums."

Blorg's eyes were wide with interest.

"All you have to do is go over to the dog and say the word ‚Sugar-Plum!" Christopher said.

"That's it? Then what happens?" Blorg asked.

"Then he barks," added Jaden.

"Yeah, that makes the chocolate cat up in the tree jump around." said Kyra, "and that's when all the Sugar-Plums fall to the ground."

"There's no other way to get them down Blorg. No matter how strong you are," informed Nod.

"So go give it a try," encouraged Wynken.

"OK," Blorg stood up and started to walk toward the Gingerbread dog, but Blorg's big size made the dog scurry away. Blorg frowned, "He runs away." He lowered his eyes to the ground, "He's afraid of me. I guess I can't do it. It's just impossible,"

Kyra stepped right up, "Don't say that Blorg. It's only impossible if you think it's impossible. Take it back and try again."

"But it is impossible. I'm just too big." Blorg dropped his head again.

"No Blorg, nothing's impossible. Think about it. Before tonight, you would have thought it's impossible for you to have seven new friends; but look, you do. So come on, believe in yourself. Take it back and try again," Kyra insisted.

Blorg took a deep breath, „OK" he answered.

"Hey Blorgy," Wynken chimed in, "Why don't you try crawling over to the gingerbread dog. Maybe if you were closer to the ground, the little guy might not scurry away."

"I am not Little!" Zook blurted out, "Oh sorry, automatic reaction."

"Go ahead Blorg, try," Kyra encouraged.

Blorg got down on all fours and crawled slowly over to the dog. This time he didn't scurry away. He wagged his tail and cocked his head in a curious tilt. When Blorg got close enough to him he said, "Sugar-Plum."

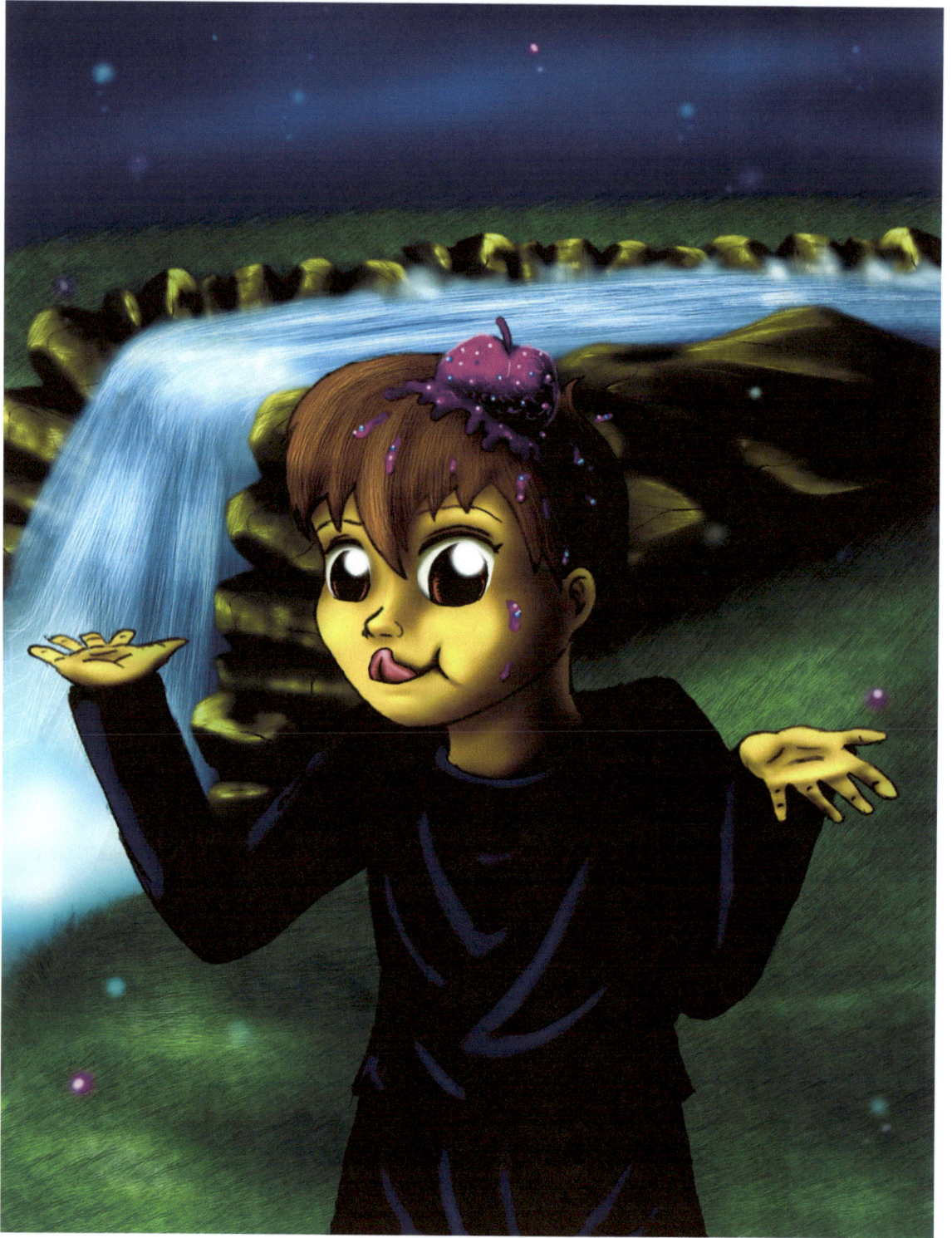

The dog made a little whine, as if double checking.

"Say it again!" said Kyra.

"Sugar-Plum" Blorg said a little louder. Then the dog barked. He barked and barked. The chocolate cat up in the tree began to jump around and the Sugar-Plums began to fall.

"You did it!" they all cheered!

As the treasures rained down from the Sugar-Plum Tree, Blorg's smile turned into laughter, and seeing Blorg so happy made everyone feel happy. Blessed in the happiness of their friendship, they all laughed and cheered, playing in the magic of the falling Sugar-Plums. It was quite funny when one of the Sugar-Plums landed with a splat on Christopher's head. The juice dripped down his cheeks. Sticking out his tongue as far as he could, Christopher licked it up. "Mmmm." he said, "That's yummy."

"Look," exclaimed Kyra as she pointed up to a top branch, "that purple gumdrop is about to fall. Who can catch it?"

Everyone took their positions to try and catch the gumdrop.

When the cat jumped to the branch, she jumped so hard, that the gumdrop flew up and over. Blorg stepped backwards, trying to catch it, but tripped. There was a big splash and water went flying everywhere as he landed in the crystal river.

"Well, he needed a bath anyway," said Zook.

Blorg was soaked. Sitting in the water, dripping wet, but triumphantly holding the purple gumdrop. While everyone was laughing and cheering at the good catch, Blorg stood up and shook himself dry. When everyone turned around again to look at Blorg, they all gasped.

"Oh my," Blynken said astonished. "Look at him!"

"What?" Blorg asked, "Why are you all looking at me so strangely?"

"Wow," said Kyra in amazement, "Blorg, you're so beautiful!"

It was true. Standing in the moonlight, clean and dry, Blorg was beautiful. He had the most gorgeous snow white fur. As thick as a cushy blanket and soft as silk. Now that he was clean and all the dirt washed off, his fur shimmered in the moonlight and flowed in the breeze. "I am?" he asked, smiling at the compliment. When he smiled it was hard to even remember how scary he looked before. He wasn't scary at all anymore.

"Hey guys, we better get back to the shoe." Wynken instructed as he stuffed his mouth with a pink marshmallow ball. "Hey big guy, can we have our shoe back?"

"Of course. I was even going to try and fix it for you, but I don't know how," replied Blorg.

"That's right. There's a hole in it. It can't sail with a hole," exclaimed Nod.

"How can we fix the shoe?" asked Kyra.

Through a mouthful of Gum drop and chocolate, Jaden cried out the answer.

"We can just stick a sugar plum in it!" They all laughed in agreement.

"Excellent idea Jaden!" Nod said.

"Come on! Hop on board!" Blorg said as he lowered his hands. Everyone jumped on, and Blorg carried everyone back to the wooden shoe.

When they arrived, Jaden stuck a big Sugar-Plum in the hole of the shoe and it held tightly.

"I think it will work!" declared Wynken. "Blorg, can you help us get the shoe in the water again?"

"Of course. Everyone get in and I'll carry the shoe down to the sea," Blorg lifted everyone in the shoe and carried them down to the shore. He eased the wooden shoe back into the water, and gave them a little nudge to start them on their way.

"Thanks Blorg!" They all called.

"Hey Blorg, I'll swim by tomorrow and bring you a toothbrush!" Zook said with a smile and a wave.

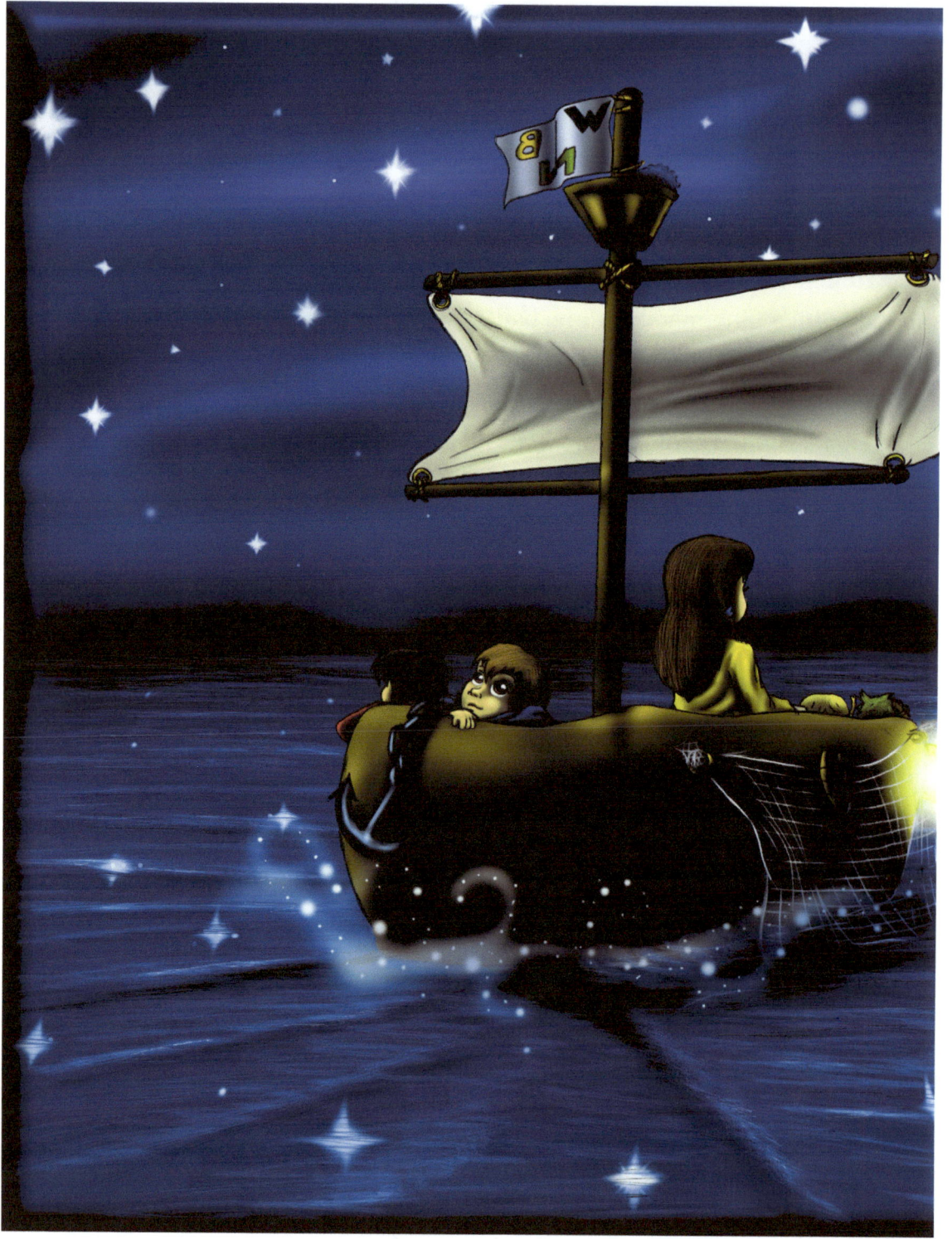

"Great!" Blorg answered. "Bye everyone. I'm glad you're my friends. I hope I see you all again soon."

As they continued to wave and say goodbye, the shoe began to sail quickly down the water, heading for home, leaving Blorg and the Island for some other day.

Eventually, the time came for Zook to part ways with the shoe and it's crew, for his world was here in the magical waters, not with them back home.
With a wave of their hands, and a wave of his fin; a flip through the air and a sly little grin, Zook splashed into the sea and was gone.

Wynken, Blynken and Nod got busy at the steering wheel of the wooden shoe making sure they were set to sail for home. Kyra, Jaden and Christopher all felt sad at the thought of leaving the wondrous world they had found.

"Was any of this real?" asked Kyra.

"Can we ever come back?" asked Christopher.

"Will we ever see Zook and Blorg again?" asked Jaden.

The Moon smiled down at them.

"Some folks think this is only a dream...some know otherwise. What I can promise you is there is always a way to come back. You must only know one thing. Do you know who Wynken, Blynken and Nod really are?" The Moon asked. "Know this, and you will forever know your way back here."
Kyra crinkled her nose in confusion. Christopher and Jaden did the same. The Moon smiled at their confusion.

"I'm sure I will see you again. Until that time, be happy, and believe."

And with that, the Moon blew a breeze of sparkles and lights that swept the wooden shoe along on its way.

"Goodbye, for now" said the Moon.

"Hey," called Wynken from the front of the boat, "We can still do some fishing on the way back!"

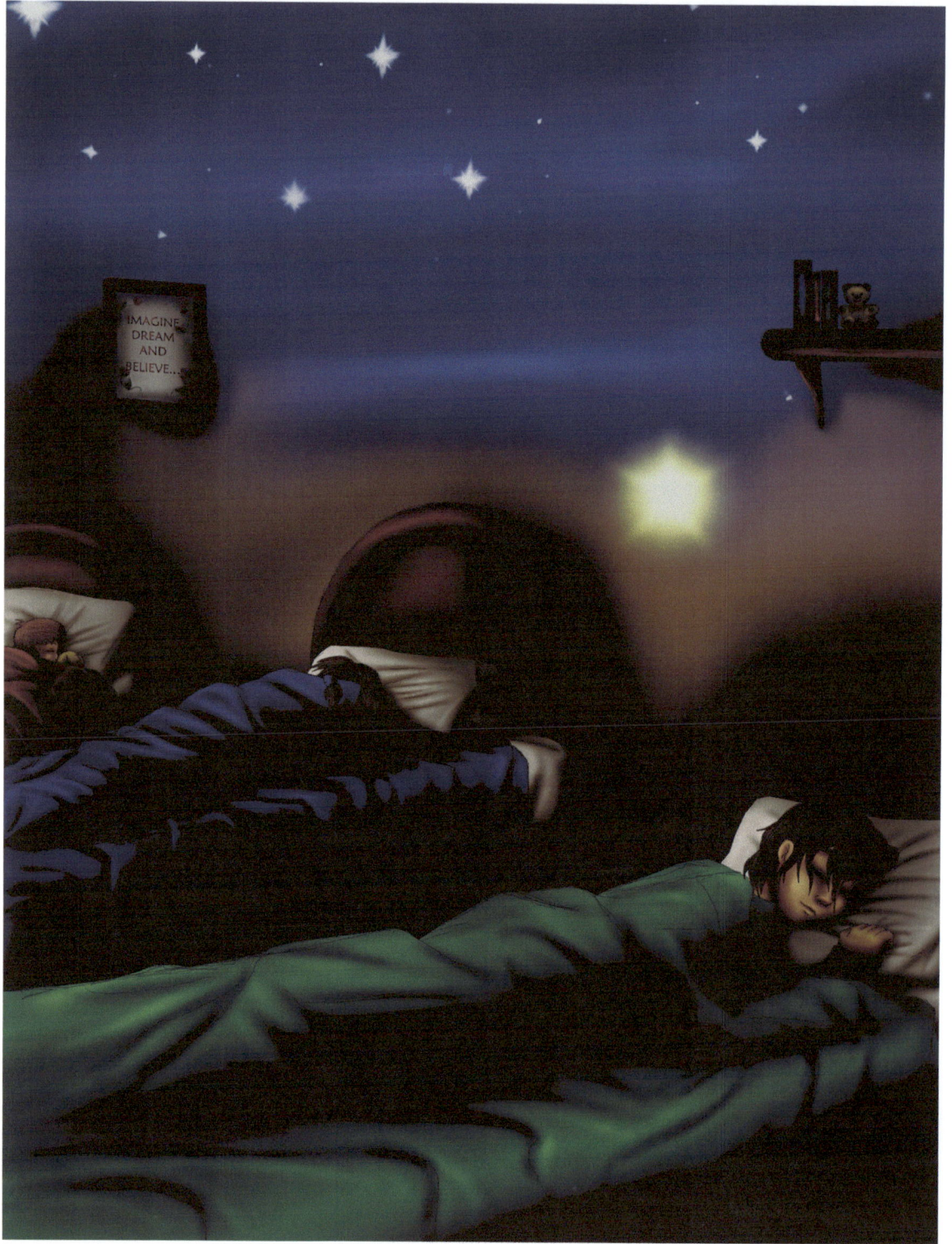

Yeah, maybe we can finally catch one," said Nod as he peered over the edge of the shoe to the sparkling reflections in the water.

The little 'fish' simply laughed and sang out with confidence,

"Never afeared are we!"

Wynken, Blynken and Nod one night
Sailed off in a wooden shoe
Sailed on a river of crystal light
Into a sea of dew

"Where are you going and what do you wish?"
The old moon asked the three
"We have come with our silver-gold nets,
To fish in your beautiful sea"
Replied the fishermen three
Wynken, Blynken & Nod

The old moon laughed and sang a song
As they rocked in their wooden shoe
And the wind that sped them all night long
Ruffled the waves of dew

The stars in the sky were the Herring fish
Sought by the fishermen three
"So cast your nets where ever you wish,
Never afeared are we!"
They sang to the fishermen three
Wynken, Blynken & Nod...

All night long their nets they threw
To the stars in the twinkling foam
Then down from the sky came the wooden shoe
Bringing the fishermen home
Twas all too pretty a sail it seemed
As if it just could not be
And some folks think, twas only a dream they dreamed
Of sailing that beautiful sea
But I shall name you the fishermen three

Wynken and Blynken are two little eyes
And Nod is a little head
And the wooden shoe that sailed the skies
Is a wee one's own little bed

So close your eyes as I sing
Of wonderful sights that be
And you shall see the most marvelous things
And sail that magical sea
Just like the fishermen three
Wynken, Blynken and Nod

Lyn Liechty

Lyn Liechty has recorded and performed the hit duet **"Here In My Heart"** with the world renowned Scorpions off the platinum selling album **"Moment Of Glory."** She has also created a big name for herself performing leading roles in world premiere blockbuster shows such as **"Jekyll & Hyde," "Dance Of The Vampires," "Miss Saigon,"** and **"Dracula."** She has worked closely with Lionel Richie, Roman Polanski, Jim Steinman, Frank Wildhorn and Leslie Bricusse to name a few. Lyn's first single **"CaveMan!"** off her album "At Last", has gotten over 1.6 million views on YouTube, and charted at #11 on the Billboard hot Singles Charts.
Lyn is the author of several books including **Winter Mountain**, **Hollywood Fire**, **Delta Rise**, **A Wynken, Blynken & Nod Adventure** (Children's book,) **The Magic Of Poems, The Magic Of Night** (Children's poems,) and two cookbooks; **Recipes Of Home** (**The Main Collection** and **Sweets Treats and Desserts**.)
For more info, please go to:

www.LynLiechtyMusic.com

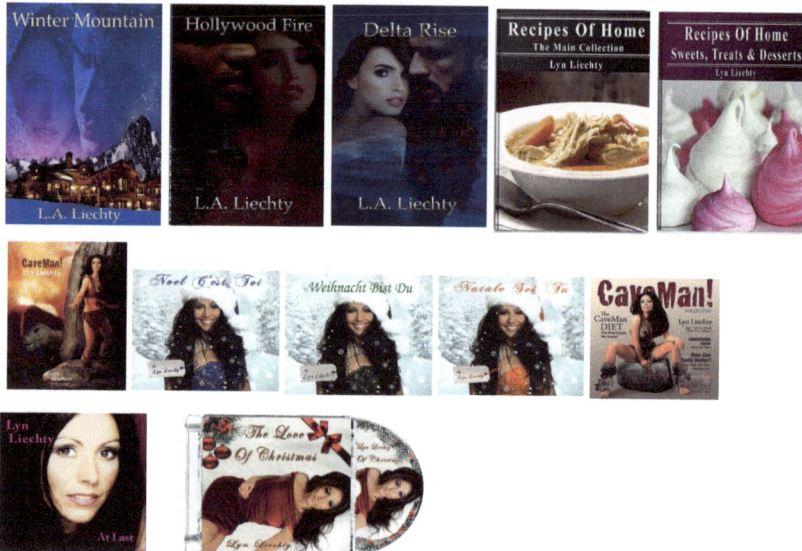

www.ingramcontent.com/pod-product-compliance
Lightning Source LLC
Chambersburg PA
CBHW042014090426
42811CB00015B/1640